Faithworks

STEVE CHALKE

KINGSWAY PUBLICATIONS

EASTBOURNE

Contents

Acknowledgements 6

Foreword 7

The *Faithworks Campaign* Declaration 12

1. Seize the Day 13

2. Faith Works 24

3. Faith in the Future 47

4. A Two-Way Street 67

Getting Involved in the *Faithworks Campaign* 90

Further Information 93

Acknowledgements

Thanks to Paul Hansford, who has burnt the candle at both ends to provide the manuscript of this book with me. And to Jane Green, Libby Barrett, Tom Jackson, Fiona Smith, Alan Mann, Jonathan Dutton, Dave Hitchcock, Jeremy Cooke, Simon Downham, Aredi Pitsiaeli, Tina Millen, James Griffin and Cornelia Chalke for the many hours and endless ideas they have contributed, as together we have developed, not only this book, but also the whole *Faithworks Campaign*.

Foreword

Purpose

The purpose of God is to make all things new. He does not treat creation like an empty plastic cup that is thrown away after use. He is for ever renewing his creation. Even when things go wrong he works to redeem the errors, just as an artist never uses an eraser but works the stray line into the drawing. Regeneration lies at the heart of God's redemptive purposes for his world.

Personal worth

Each person on the face of the earth is created in God's image and of infinite worth. There is nobody beyond the pale of God's love. We have been made to relate to God and to each other. The recovery of our self-esteem and the restoration of our relationships with God and each other are central to the regenerating work of God in his world.

Power to change

The Christian faith is based upon the claim of Jesus Christ to hold the power to change and transform both individuals and communities. Regeneration has to be more than economic, material and physical; it must also be social, moral and spiritual. The antidote to poor self-esteem is to know that you are loved. The experience of God's love in Jesus is affirming and transforming.

Prayer

To pray for the coming of God's kingdom means opening yourself up to the possibility of God changing your own life personally and individually, and changing the structures that hold people back and oppress them. The values of God's kingdom are derived from the virtues of God's character, who as the God of love is full of justice and mercy. God's kingdom is both the church and the world. Christians have by the grace of God had their eyes and hearts opened to see and acknowledge the reign of God in their lives. But the world is also God's kingdom, for there is not one centimetre of it that can be removed from the sovereignty of God. In the Lord's Prayer we pray 'Your kingdom come' and look to God to establish his rule of justice and mercy over the whole world.

Practical faith

Those who follow Christ are called to match their words of faith with deeds of love. Faith without works is dead and no use to anyone. We cannot say that we love God and then ignore our neighbour. Christians are under an obligation to work their faith out in practice and to show God's love to the world as a servant community to the wider community.

Partners

We will often find ourselves as partners with people of other denominations, of other faiths and of no faith at all. We will work with all those God has chosen to advance the cause of justice. The Cyrus factor means that God can choose anyone to work out his purposes. Let those who are not against us work with us and us with them to care for the poor and empower the voiceless.

Prophetic

We have a prophetic calling to declare the values of God's kingdom. This imposes upon us a responsibility to show those very values in the quality of our community life. It is by our life as much as by our words that we reveal the nature of God's kingdom.

Political

There is inevitably a political dimension to all that we do. Leaders of Christian communities are pastors and not politicians or economists. However, as pastors we often see the consequences of public policy and are called by God through the Bible to speak up for the poor and the powerless so that public policy might change.

Peace

Peace and wholeness are God's plan for his creation. The pic-
ture that comes constantly to mind when thinking about the
renewal of our cities and communities is that of Jesus standing outside Jerusalem and weeping, saying, 'If only you
knew the things that make for peace. . .' Over the years many
people have suggested solutions to the problems in the inner
cities and outer estates. Unfortunately, most of those solutions have been prescribed by people who live outside those
areas. The people who really know the things that make for
peace are those who live within the community. They know
the problems and they know the solutions.

The *Faithworks Campaign* is a challenge and an encouragement to local Christians to be intimately involved in their
local communities. When we are, then we are able to match
our actions with our words and say something about how
God is alongside the least, the last and the lost. It is about
helping everybody to know that however damaged we may
be we still bear the marks of God's image and are infinitely
valuable in his sight. It is about the poor rediscovering their
own potential and experiencing a power from another
source to shape their own future, both for their own good
and for the glory of God.

In Chinese the word for 'crisis' is made up of two characters: danger and opportunity. There are dangerous levels of
unemployment, educational under-achievement, drug
abuse, youth alienation, poor health and crime. There is danger in our cities. But there is also opportunity. It is the oppor-

tunity of redemption and regeneration. It is summed up in the Nazareth Manifesto, where Jesus speaks about what it means to be truly anointed by the Spirit; 'To preach good news to the poor. . . to proclaim freedom for the prisoners and recovery of sight for the blind, to release the oppressed, to proclaim the year of the Lord's favour' (Luke 4:18–19).

The Rt Rev James Jones, the Bishop of Liverpool
November 2000

The *Faithworks Campaign* Declaration

The *Faithworks Campaign* calls on the incoming government:

1. To recognize the important contribution that local churches and Christian charities have made and can make in providing welfare within the local community.

2. To acknowledge the vital role that faith plays in the motivation and effectiveness of welfare programmes developed by churches and Christian charities.

3. To encourage and support the work of local initiatives developing welfare in the community, including those run by churches and other faith-based organizations, through specific legislation, outcome-related monitoring and funding without unnecessary bureaucracy or cost.

4. To ensure that funding criteria for government and local authority grants to projects providing welfare in the local community do not discriminate against the faith that is vital to the success of the work of churches and faith-based organizations.

1. Seize the Day

'There are three things I don't like about you.' The then head of the Council Housing Department wasn't a man to mince his words. I'd just outlined our plan to set up a small, referred-access hostel for homeless young people in his borough, and he was somewhat underwhelmed by our proposal, to say the least.

'First,' he explained, sneering at me as I sat in his office, 'you're a Christian. Second, you're an *Evangelical* Christian.' After these two I wondered what would come next. 'Third,' he announced, 'you're a minister. We don't need any hostels run by your type around here. If you open, it'll be over my dead body!'

I don't know what happened to him, but we did open. It took over four years to turn our vision into a reality, but we managed it. And Oasis, the charity I started over 15 years ago with the specific aim of opening that one hostel, now runs a range of different facilities for homeless people in London's inner city.

And our approach works: figures from that first hostel

show that around 80 per cent of the young people who've stayed there and then been 'resettled' by us have held down a job and stayed in housing for at least three years after leaving us. They're making a contribution to the community around them rather than remaining the 'victims' of society.

What's more, in spite of the vehement protests of that Head of Housing over a decade ago, the local council is now in absolutely no doubt just how good a job we do. A senior representative of that same London borough council admitted to me recently that our resettlement figures were impressive – in fact, they were ones he wished other hostels on his patch could emulate.

Yet amazingly we still find ourselves constantly facing religious discrimination. Sometimes the element of faith gets deliberately left out of the equation, shunted carefully out of the limelight like an embarrassing relative. Many of our projects have been praised by local statutory bodies, but always in terms that take no account whatsoever of the fact that we're a faith-based charity. Just as often, however, we've found that our faith has positively counted against us. All of our homeless facilities struggle to find enough money to meet their modest running costs, for example, and yet bureaucracy has blocked statutory funding to us time and again simply because we're a specifically Christian agency.

And we're far from alone. Faith-based agencies of all kinds, especially Christian ones, tend to find themselves being effectively discriminated against purely on the grounds of their religious convictions. For a whole host of reasons – from the groundless suspicion that all Christian care is really just a covert attempt at church 'recruitment' to straightforward anti-Christian prejudice – a great many churches and Christian charities find themselves constantly having to 'hide their light under a bushel' in their dealings with local statutory bodies. In effect, they're forced to choose between either massively downplaying their religious core and commitment, or missing out on taking a vital stake in local community action. They risk losing both opportunities for partnership and vital funds and resources from local authorities.

We've never engaged in any underhanded attempts at proselytism, nor have we in any way foisted our beliefs on our residents or clients – though, by the same token, we've never tried to conceal them. But to our staff of committed Christians, faith has always been a very powerful source of both motivation and inspiration. If you asked any of them why they were prepared to work long hours for comparatively little pay, and why their job gave them such enjoyment, their faith would come at the very top of their list of reasons.

On the threshold of a century of opportunity, ours is a society with no more vision of where it is going than those stumbling home early on New Year's Day. The Dome is a fitting national symbol, a wonderful structure that stands for nothing, a stunning shell with a hole where the heart should be.
The Times, 1st January 2000

Why, then, should one of the key things that makes us so

effective, and has helped us establish such a good track record as a care provider, be an embarrassment or an impediment when it comes to getting recognition, respect and vital resources? Why are local councils, and some other governmental organizations, still suspicious of the role that our faith plays in our work? Why should we have to de-emphasize our Christian ethos and vision when it's such an integral part of who we are?

Faith works

It's faith that drives churches and Christian charities up and down the UK to get involved in care and welfare provision in the first place. It's faith that pushes us to develop a clearer understanding of the massively complex problems at issue within society, and to strive for more effective medium- and long-term solutions. It's faith that motivates us to keep going when the going gets tough and the mission ahead looks impossible.

In short, it's faith that compels us, in the famous words of St Francis of Assisi, to work to 'sow love where there is hatred, pardon where there is injury, faith where there is doubt, hope where there is despair, light where there is darkness, and joy where there is sadness'.

Social reform is about far more than resources and externals. Real change comes from within. The greatest poverty our nation faces is a poverty of hope. That's why Christian faith is potent. Faith transforms lives, and that's why faith *works*.

Faith isn't just a key motivator for people to get involved in projects linked to welfare provision; it's also a key motivator for them to stay involved in these projects. What's more, it helps to ensure that their involvement is the kind that produces genuine long-term creative outcomes: positive, professional, practical, personal and persevering.

Faith-based agencies, by their very nature as faith-based agencies, are watermarked by five characteristics that are essential components in any meaningful, realistic approach to care and welfare provision. The care they offer is:

Rooted

Faith-based agencies, especially churches, aren't just local, they're also firmly rooted to specific geographical communities. They're a permanent part of those communities, 24 hours a day and 365 days a year. They don't clock off at 5 p.m. – they're there for the long haul. And that means they not only come face to face with all the problems and needs of their community, day after day, but they also have to live with the reality of all those problems and needs themselves – not to mention the consequences of the various approaches taken to solve them! Churches and other faith-based groups therefore have a real depth of insight into their local community, and a vested interest in improving its welfare on both the pastoral and practical fronts.

Sustainable

Because they're locally rooted, churches and other faith-based groups necessarily take a long-term view of the problems and needs of their area. They know that the 'quick-fix' approach doesn't work. All too often, they've seen the disastrous results of the 'here today gone tomorrow' attitude taken by too many organizations in the past, including local or perhaps even national governments more worried about elections than real results, as well as various well-meaning but badly informed quangos (quasi-autonomous non-governmental organizations). In most cases, 'quick-fix' solutions have created more harm than good. As a result, local churches are striving for real, workable medium- and long-term solutions.

Committed

One of the key differences between an effective charity organization and an ineffective one is the motivation levels of its staff and volunteers. The sheer scale and complexity of the issues faced by most voluntary sector groups offering care and welfare is totally daunting. Tackling the same, seemingly insurmountable, problems day after day can seem about as worthwhile and sensible as trying to turn back the tide. The advances and achievements that do happen seem so tiny by comparison with the task still to be done. To keep going in the face of wave after wave of what can frequently appear to be nothing more than constant setback and futility requires deep reserves of energy and vision – reserves that are an integral part of faith.

Imaginative

One of the major side effects of having high levels of commitment and a real faith in the future, however, is a constant determination to find new ways around or over obstacles. *Stupidity is doing what you did yesterday again today and expecting a different result.* Faith breeds a can-do culture, and a can-do culture refuses to see any obstacle as final. For Christians, not even death is the end of the story.

God, not injustice or 'impossibility', has the last word. As a result, faith-based groups such as local churches approach problems with both optimism and imagination. They're not naïve – most are all too aware of their limitations – but they are committed to being as flexible and imaginative as possible, determined not to give up until they've found a way round a problem, or removed it entirely. Our commitment to constantly seeking innovative ways forward springs from our understanding of the principle of incarnation, the very core of our faith. God became one of us. He inventively accommodated himself to our culture in order to meet our needs.

Transforming

Poverty isn't just a material problem; it's a spiritual one as well. Personal, internal change is an essential ingredient in real social transformation. Throwing money at social deprivation can only ever provide temporary solutions to the problems confronting our society. That's why Christian faith is so potent: it develops the strength and health of both individuals and communities. Put simply, faith sparks transformation. Churches, aware that every individual is made in the image of God and personally loved by him, are highly motivated to give them the individual time, respect and dignity that no administrative system can ever offer. People begin to believe in themselves when they know that someone else believes in them. And when people begin to grasp their own importance and value as individuals, not only are they transformed, but they also help to transform others. The wheels of genuine social transformation begin to turn.

In Britain, the Judaeo–Christian foundation to our society has played a key role in fashioning the social concern that becomes the welfare state. But we are mistaken if we think we can subcontract the social concern and compassion demanded by our faith to the state and simply leave it there. There is a growing recognition that the state can do many things well, but it cannot deliver the personal or spiritual support that we all need to overcome life's greatest adversities.

Gary Streeter, MP

Actions speak louder than words

We now stand at the threshold of an enormous opportunity. In the run-up to the General Election, the major political parties are beginning to sing from the same song sheet. They're talking about the need for greater involvement by different voluntary groups, including churches and Christian charities, in providing welfare to those on the margins of society.

In July 2000, both Prime Minister Tony Blair and Conservative Leader William Hague took time out of their schedules to address 'Faith in the Future', the millennium conference of the UK's black-majority churches. Both men praised the vital role that black churches have played in rejuvenating not just black culture, but British culture as a whole. What's more, they recognized the role that black-majority churches, and other churches, will play in the future in the areas of education, employment and community development.

Blair spoke of how black-majority churches have been

active in 'enriching' and 're-energizing' society. He welcomed the interest many black churches had shown in setting up 'City Academies' – state-funded, independently run secondary schools. 'Faith communities have an important part to play in this,' he told delegates. Hague was just as strong. 'There is plenty of evidence that inner-city children who are involved with their local church have a much greater chance of escaping poverty and drug addiction. The work that churches have been doing on strengthening families, teaching parenting skills, and micro-employment projects gives us a clear idea of the way we should go,' he remarked. 'Your churches stand as shining lights of hope in communities which feel disadvantaged and discriminated against.'

There is, however, still a massive gap between the rhetoric and the reality. At present, there are no clear policies or concrete proposals to ensure these good intentions are matched in practice.

The truth of this was hammered home to me after a very positive meeting with staff in Downing Street about the possibility of setting up a City Academy. The supportive attitude of Westminster's corridors of power seemed to evaporate the moment we crossed the river and started dealing with the London borough in which we actually planned to run the school. The language of support gave way to the language of suspicion. In marked contrast to the warm and enthusiastic response we'd received from the different parliamentary political parties, the local council saw our Christian faith and foundation as a real problem.

It is to bridge this gap between rhetoric and reality that

Oasis has launched *Faithworks* – not just this book, but a whole *Faithworks Campaign* aimed at putting in place concrete structures on the ground to ensure that faith-based groups (Christian and otherwise) aren't allowed to be the continued victims of religious discrimination when it comes to welfare provision initiatives. We're not asking for favoured status, just a level playing field. From homelessness to health care, from job clubs to children's clubs, from back-up for young parents to care for elderly grandparents – local churches and Christian charities throughout the UK demonstrate seven days a week, 365 days a year, that *faith works*. But in borough after borough, council after council, quango after quango, we find ourselves being discriminated against simply because of the role played by our faith.

Faith is good, not bad. It's progressive, not regressive. It's empowering, not enslaving. Our faith is a genuine asset, not a liability, when it comes to providing best quality, cost-effective care. Faith is the engine that drives the church's work. So our message to government is: *Don't remove our engine!* Don't let other people's prejudice force us to behave as if our faith isn't a vital, life-giving part of who and what we are. For us at least, no faith, no works. Let our records speak for themselves. Rather than hampering our efforts by forcing us to downplay the importance of our faith, help us by recognizing that it's a major key to our success. It lies at the heart of our motivation and effectiveness as care providers. Don't rob us of this essential ingredient. Don't make us act like agnostics to gain your confidence or respect.

That's why our message to our political leaders and representatives – whoever wins the next General Election – is simple: you talk a great game, but we've yet to see this translated into reality. It's time to put your muscle (and your money) where your mouth is.

2. Faith Works

Faith has a key public role to play.

Churches and Christian charities offer more than just help and a handout. They offer true hope and humanity. As Christians, we're committed to bringing about real, lasting change in individuals and in society *because* of our faith in a God of unconditional love and justice, not *despite* it. The content and character of our faith directly affects the content and character of the care we give.

In short, our faith is the source of our vision and vitality. It drives us. It gives us more empathy, a better understanding of the problems, higher motivation and a firm commitment to stay with it through thick and thin, 'for better or worse'. Our faith cannot simply be strained off to leave some purer substance. Our faith is our vital ingredient. For the church at least, no faith means no works!

For churches and Christian charities involved in welfare provision, exactly the same is true of the relationship between our faith and our action. Faith and action form two sides of the same coin that gives our work its strength and sustainability. You can't have one without the other. Take away the element of faith and the result becomes fundamentally unsound and unworkable; the project loses the vital balance, support and motivation it gets from faith.

As part of our ongoing work with homeless people, Oasis set up the Oasis Health Centre. Unique in south London, it combines medical consultation with chiropody, haircuts and free coffee, and what our clients themselves describe as 'the best showers in London'. Report after report has praised the unit for its professionalism, provision and popularity among London's rough sleepers. Our staff, we're told, are courteous and considerate, with a high level of motivation. Our volunteers – high-level doctors, expert chiropodists, experienced hairdressers – are enthusiastic, committed and professional. Our support network – local churches and youth groups that keep us stocked up with blankets, clothes and other essential good-quality second-hand items – is enviable. Our commercial sponsorship (companies that generously supply us with gifts in kind) is noteworthy. And our track record – 12,500 consultations a year, which works out at almost 50 a day – is impressive for a modest-sized institution. These, we're told, are the key ingredients that make the Oasis Health Centre a top-notch care unit.

Yet never has an official report thought to ask *why* our staff are considerate and highly motivated, *why* our volunteers (despite busy schedules) are enthusiastic and committed, *why* our support network works so hard, and *why* companies want to get behind what we're doing with generous donations of much-needed resources. If they looked closer, they'd see that all these things are simply the effects of the cause, and the cause is our faith.

The problem is, a great many 'secular' institutions and statutory bodies look at what we do and assume, wrongly, that our faith is a kind of bolt-on extra. More often than not it's a bolt-on extra they'd really rather bolt off. But the truth is that our faith is fundamental to our work. It's our faith that works.

It's our faith that generates the five characteristics that are essential components in any meaningful, realistic approach to welfare provision. It's our faith that ensures that the care we provide is:

- rooted
- sustainable
- committed
- imaginative
- transforming.

The work of the Church is for the whole community, not just those who go to services. That is why we are active seven days a week, not just Sundays. That is why we are there for all citizens, whether they are Christian or not.
George Carey, Archbishop of Canterbury

1. Rooted

A decade ago, when Oasis outgrew its headquarters in the front room of one of our London hostels, we moved into small offices above a local inner-city church. It was a *quid pro quo* arrangement: in return for vital office space, we provided the tiny church with much-needed office skills and staff. As a result, we soon found ourselves branching out into the unexpected. In particular, because we were now not just a small charity but were also acting as a local church, we found ourselves undergoing a crash course in finding out just how to help local people get the state benefits they were entitled to.

In an area of high unemployment and low education, many local residents found the benefits system completely baffling. It's hardly surprising – we found it baffling too, and our staff included a former senior civil servant fluent in the language of bureaucracy. If *he* couldn't understand it, what chance did the rest of us have? As he put it, 'Even Einstein would have had trouble!'

Unsure of exactly what they were entitled to or how to get it, many locals turned to the church for help. I'd like to say that our skills, sensitivity and spiritual integrity made us the obvious choice, but the truth is that we were by and large the *only* choice. People had nowhere else to turn. Most of the staff in the benefits office tried to be as helpful as they could, but they tended to lack not only the time but sometimes also the necessary expertise or authority to guide people through the long and complicated process of making a correct claim.

What Oasis and that tiny church offered local people was something they could never get from the massive, impersonal state machine: a friendly human face. We didn't make them feel stupid for not understanding all of the ins and outs of the paperwork. We helped to steer them patiently and painstakingly through the baffling bureaucratic maze. And we stood up for them and supported them during all the trials and traumas of getting the various state benefits they were entitled to by law.

It was something we could do because we were small, flexible and local enough to be able to respond to individual need with individual attention. We didn't have scores of benefits lawyers up our sleeves or massive amounts of expertise in benefits application. But what made people on the nearby housing estates turn to us for help was that we were local, we were there, and we had time to give individual care, attention and respect.

A century or two ago, the church stood at the centre of each community, literally. In most towns or villages, the architectural centrepiece was a large church building right next to a bustling marketplace. In most cities, a cathedral was centre stage, the tallest and grandest building for miles around. The priest or pastor was one of the central figures in the local community.

Today, church spires and bell towers are dwarfed by high-rise apartment buildings and office blocks. The tallest and grandest building around is more likely to be the headquarters of a bank than a place of worship, and the essential place to be on a Sunday is more likely to be a shopping centre than a cathedral. But even though the church isn't as powerful and influential as it once was, it still tends to be there at the heart of the community. What's more, although society's understanding of the church's role may have dramatically decreased over the years, the church's understanding of its role in society is as strong as ever.

Hardly a town or village in the UK is without a church

building and a community of worshipping Christians. It's a unique network: local churches made up of local people in every corner of the land. And it's a network that makes churches the most locally rooted organizations in the country. We have more local outlets than any other corporate or voluntary body. That's a big advantage when it comes to meeting local needs. No other welfare agency has that kind of local presence, and no other welfare agency has that kind of local knowledge.

But churches aren't just geographically rooted in a local area, they're theologically rooted there too. It wasn't accident or opportunism that took missionaries to every corner of the land, but a real desire to 'incarnate' God's presence both near and far. 'The Word became flesh and made his dwelling among us,' John 1:14 tells us, explaining the incarnation. Jesus lived an anonymous life in a small, little-known Galilean village for around 30 years before stepping forward into the limelight. He spoke their language, understood their culture, laughed at their jokes and wept over their struggles. And when he finally ascended, he left in place a community dedicated to the same long-term, incarnational approach.

We usually tend to think of characters like Paul and Barnabas whenever we think of New Testament 'missionaries', but the truth is that they were the exceptions, not the rule. Most Christians, and most 'missionaries', were local people responding to the various needs, both spiritual and material (a distinction that *we* often make, but one that wouldn't actually have occurred to them). In fact, the majority of Christian men and women would have lived their entire lives, cradle to grave, in pretty much the same place. Welfare and mission don't get much more local or rooted than that.

Today, this firm commitment to local rooting can be seen even in the refusal of some of the more established denominations to close church buildings, especially in remote or deprived areas, despite rapidly increasing financial pressures and constantly decreasing congregations. Rather than shut up shop or merge tiny congregations together, these denominations have opted to retain a local presence, even if several congregations have to share a minister. It may not be the most commercially astute decision to have made, but it's part of a determined effort to 'practise the presence of Christ', as Brother Lawrence put it back in the late 1600s, in every local area in the country.

And it's a commitment that can pay real dividends in terms of more than infrastructure. Because churches are there, and there to stay, they can have a real depth of insight into the problems of people in the local area, and a vested interest in supporting everything that truly promotes both community and individual welfare. They don't go home at the end of the day – they're already home.

They're driven by a theological mandate to be 'salt and light' to those around them: preserving, flavouring and enlightening their local communities.

Voluntary organizations have a long and proud history of identifying new needs, pioneering fresh solutions, often cajoling governments into action, often long before government has admitted that there is a problem.
Gordon Brown, Chancellor of the Exchequer

Our faith, therefore, plays an integral part in ensuring that our care is more effective by remaining locally rooted.

2. Sustainable

When the Indian state of Maharashtra was devastated by an earthquake in 1993, killing over 25,000 people in just 43 seconds, the government responded to the ensuing crisis by building several new villages in what seemed to be ideal locations. But today they stand empty and unused, ghost towns in the middle of nowhere.

The reason? Like so many initiatives by so many governments in so many countries, including our own, they were 'quick-fix' solutions. Unfortunately, ministers were so sure of the rightness of their approach that they didn't stop to consult with local people. As a result, for all the right reasons they did what turned out to be entirely the wrong thing.

An alternative approach was taken by the Emmanuel Hospital Association (EHA). Working alongside Oasis and GMTV, which raised around three-quarters of a million pounds for a hospital project, the EHA carefully listened to local needs before acting. Local people soon took it to heart, and staff learned how to ensure that the care they provided was the care people needed. Today, that hospital has not only opened its own thriving school, but a village has grown up around it.

I don't tell this story to criticize the Indian government. But having seen with my own eyes the stark contrast between the thriving, bustling GMTV Priya Hospital and the totally deserted government-built villages, I'm only too aware of the dangers of taking short cuts when it comes to providing welfare for those who are most vulnerable in our society.

The truth is, quick fixes simply don't work. When tragedy strikes, it can often seem urgent and vital to be doing something to help, but if that something isn't the *right* thing, it can all too easily turn out in the end to have been a disastrous waste of time and resources. That's why it's so crucial for us to take a long-term view of both the problems encountered by those around us – especially those on the margins of society – and the various proposals being put forward as to how to solve those problems.

Partly because they're permanently there, and partly because they've seen the success or failure of a number of past initiatives, churches and local Christian charities are well placed to help formulate realistic and workable solutions for the future.

The fact is, poverty isn't a problem you can solve overnight, or by simply throwing money at it. Poverty needs solutions that aren't imposed by a remote authority, but arise from amid the people themselves – solutions they own, because they're tailored to their exact needs and allow them to grow at their own pace. Poverty needs solutions that work from the bottom up, not the top down; solutions that *e*volve and *in*volve.

Churches and other Christian organizations are well placed to innovate and implement these kinds of solutions, because they're already in place and they understand as an article of their faith that real social change takes time, and that it never happens without a personal, individual transformation happening alongside it.

Government can do certain things very well, but it cannot put
hope in our hearts or a sense of purpose in our lives. That
requires churches and synagogues and mosques and charities.

George W. Bush, Texas Governor and 2000 US
Presidential Candidate

3. Committed

Amazed at her tireless work among the children of a
Calcutta slum, a journalist once asked Mother Teresa how
she coped with seeing so much tragedy, so much need,
every single day. The problems of the slum seemed so
immense, and so completely insoluble, and her resources
seemed so meagre by comparison, that the journalist was
at a total loss to understand why the ageing Yugoslavian
nun didn't just throw up her hands in despair and retire,
gracefully, to the Costa Brava.

'How do you feed all those children?' she asked.

Mother Teresa's reply was disarmingly simple: 'One at a
time.'

The problems of poverty and welfare provision are massive. And it's not just the scale of the problems that's daunting, but their complexity as well. One problem feeds into
another, tangled up like strands of spaghetti on a plate. Just
when you think you've finally solved one, another two or
three present themselves, and you find you can't actually
solve the one until you've solved all the others, and you
can't solve the others until you've solved the one. It's a real
catch-22 scenario. As a result, it's completely spiritually,
emotionally, physically and intellectually draining.

In the face of such impossible problems, maintaining a high level of motivation means having both a positive perspective and a constant source of spiritual and emotional renewal. It therefore seems strange and short-sighted that many local authorities and statutory bodies are so suspicious of the role that faith plays in motivating and sustaining both Christian and other faith-based agencies. After all, faith is one of the prime sources in life for vision, inspiration and spiritual sustenance.

The irony is, of course, that not only was the sincerity and effectiveness of Mother Teresa's faith and welfare work plain for all to see, but the connection between the two could not have been clearer. Few of those who constantly object to the explicit faith of churches and other Christian groups when providing respect or resources for care projects would ever dare to question Mother Teresa's integrity on either front. Why, then, do they constantly doubt the possibility of committed Christians providing welfare care with integrity and professionalism?

The answer, I think, is that they make a stark division between faith, on the one hand, and 'fact' on the other. Before his recent death, I was privileged to become friends with the theologian and long-term missionary to India, Lesslie Newbigin. Our conversations ranged over many issues, including the way our society increasingly seems to devalue faith in general and Christian faith in particular. As we talked, he explained that the problem, as he saw it, was that religion was becoming more and more privatized. The gulf was widening, he argued, between public life, with its 'objective' facts and hard certainties, and private life, with its 'subjective' faith and designer values. It was clear to him that this would be a disaster not just for faith, but for society as a whole. He once wrote in *The Gospel in a Pluralist Society* (SPCK, 1989):

> What seems to have happened in our culture is a falling apart, a disconnection between the subjective and objective poles. We have on the one hand the ideal, or shall I call it the illusion, of a kind of objectivity which is not possible, of a kind of knowledge of what we call the 'facts' which involves no personal commitment, no risk of being wrong, something which we merely have to accept without question; and on the other hand a range of beliefs which are purely subjective, which are, as we say, 'true for me,' are 'what I feel,' but which are a matter of personal and private choice.

In other words, many of the local councils, quangos and government-financed funding bodies that object to self-confessed Christians and Christian groups being involved in welfare provision do so because they believe that faith and the rest of life have little or no connection. Christians who make an issue out of their faith, therefore, must surely have as their motive a desire to stray from the public realm of fact and physical provision (entirely appropriate for a care provider) into the private realm of faith and personal conviction (entirely inappropriate for a care provider). Since faith is a purely private and personal thing, they say, those who insist on being public about their religious beliefs must have an ulterior motive: proselytism.

The falseness of this position, of course, isn't hard to see. Not only are the 'facts' of public life nothing like so cut and dried as they imagine – just listen to two politicians arguing about 'the facts of the matter': even when they're working from the same set of statistics, they can draw wildly different interpretations of what the 'facts' really are – but 'private' faith can be, and frequently is, a real motivator and sustainer in public life.

Our faith is a genuine asset, not a liability, when it comes to providing best quality, cost-effective care. Of course this claim is contentious and unpalatable to some, but it remains a matter for debate we can't avoid without compromising our entire *raison d'être*. Political correctness and common sense aren't always the same thing.

Eric Liddell, hero of the Oscar-winning film *Chariots of Fire*, never hid the fact that he was a Christian. He was even quite blatant about the fact that his faith was a major factor in his desire to run. When he ran fast, as he usually did, lining himself up as a favourite to win gold in the 100 yards at the 1924 Paris Olympic Games, he remarked that he could 'feel God's pleasure'. Nevertheless, when he refused to compete in the qualifying heats for the race because they fell on a Sunday – a day he believed was set aside exclusively for God, not sport – the British Olympic Committee tried to get him to change his mind. Most of the committee members just couldn't see what difference it made *what* day he ran on.

Committee Chairman, the Duke of Sutherland, however, understood Liddell's drive and motivation perfectly. In the film, when a way forward is suggested (entering him for the 400 yards, a distance he'd never run at that level before, but which he went on to win in style), the Duke confides his relief to a colleague. Liddell, he says, 'is a true man of principle, and a true athlete. His speed is a mere extension of his life – his force. We sought to sever his running from himself.'

But it's not just Christianity for which the connection between private faith and public action is made explicit. Alcoholics Anonymous, the famous self-help group for those wanting to give up the bottle, is by no means an exclusively or predominantly Christian organization. Truly international, found in many countries in the world, it nevertheless recommends that all members trying to kick the habit through its Twelve Step Programme believe in a God of some description. Though it's not specific about exactly who or what its 2 million members should believe in, the organization still recognizes a fundamental connection between personal faith and the ability to change. Without faith in a 'power greater than ourselves', no real change is possible.

> *Voluntary organizations, including the churches, have a special role to play, for they have strengths that no bureaucracy can match. They mobilize hundreds of thousands of volunteers. They are responsive, locally accountable, infinitely adaptable, and put the needs of the disadvantaged before the rules of the system.*
> Michael Portillo, MP

Churches and Christian charities, in the same way, see an inherent connection between personal (but not 'private') faith and public life. We know from many centuries of experience as care providers that to keep going in the face

of wave after wave of what can often seem like nothing
more than constant setback and futility takes deep reserves
of energy and vision – reserves that are an integral part of
faith. What high achievers like Eric Liddell and Mother
Teresa knew for themselves, the rest of us just want recognized by those people in positions of power and authority
at a local level: that our faith is a vital part of our motivation and success. To have real faith in the future, you've
got to have real faith in the here-and-now.

4. Imaginative

Most of the key advances in our society, both in terms of
technology and policy, happen because of the work of individuals who are able to think 'outside the box'. They're
sufficiently far removed from established, traditional ways
of seeing a problem to be able to contribute a fresh and creative approach to solving it.

Many churches and other faith-based charities are sufficiently removed from the established central or local government approaches to problems that they can often, as
Chancellor Gordon Brown put it in a speech to charity
bosses, 'lead governments to new ways of thinking about
problems, and indeed new ways of solving them'. What's
more, they're often small and flexible enough to adapt
existing ideas and solutions so that they work a lot better.

The Peckham Evangelical Churches Action Network
(PECAN) was started in 1989 as a response by Peckham's
various Evangelical churches to the poverty and rising
unemployment in the area. Consciously trying to match
their own skills with the region's needs, they focused on

offering education and training for local unemployed people. PECAN's approach is proactive: rather than waiting for unemployed people to come to them, a handful of professional recruiters knock on every door of the estate several times a year, inviting those without a job to join an Employment Preparation Course. The four-week course is designed to help people 'smarten up' their CVs, improve their form-filling and interview skills, and, most importantly, boost their self-confidence. PECAN's success rate is more than 70 per cent, with over a third of all 'graduates' finding a job and another third going into specific job-related training.

The hard work, care and dedication of everyone in PECAN was recognized a few years ago when the Managing Director, Simon Pellew, was awarded the prestigious London Electricity 'Londoner of the Year' award in 1997.

PECAN's philosophy takes a holistic view of life. Unemployment isn't just about not having a job. The barriers that prevent people from finding work can be 'practical (such as not being able to speak English), intellectual (such as not understanding how to fill in an application form), emotional (such as the demotivation resulting from rejection after rejection) or spiritual (such as losing a sense of hope and purpose in life)'. By refusing to treat people as just more unemployment statistics, and by being flexible and imaginative enough to offer high-quality, joined-up initiatives stressing personal self-worth, PECAN has effected real social change.

But where does this philosophy come from? To put it bluntly, PECAN's basis of faith. Just because door-to-door recruiters don't thump Bibles or foist their beliefs onto vulnerable members of society doesn't mean that their Christian faith isn't an integral part of what they do and how they do it. PECAN's approach is an implicit outworking of their core Christian belief that every person in Peckham (and beyond) is special to a God whose interest and involvement in their lives doesn't stop at the doors of a church or a tick-box on a doctrinal statement. Faith isn't just a motivator. It also lies behind PECAN's imaginative and effective approach to reducing unemployment in Peckham and empowering local people.

> *From the perspective of the Bible, hope is not simply a feeling or a mood or a rhetorical flourish. Hope is the very dynamic of history. Hope is the engine of change. Hope is the energy of transformation. Hope is the door from one reality to another . . . Between impossibility and possibility, there is a door, the door of hope. And the possibility of history's transformation lies through that door . . . Real social change is . . . about releasing the aspirations of millions of people.*
> Jim Wallis, Leader of Sojourners Community

Up and down the country, countless church-based projects just as ground-breaking, integrative and effective as PECAN are making real changes for the better in our society. Their faith gives them a refreshing perspective, inspires them with real vision for the future, and enables them to devise flexible, workable, innovative and imaginative solutions to complex, deep-rooted problems. Because they're small, they're rooted, and they're driven by their belief in God's boundless love for both individuals and whole communities. They're able to 'think outside the box' and develop imaginative ways forward for the future.

5. Transforming

'The biggest disease today is not leprosy or tuberculosis,' said Mother Teresa, 'but rather the feeling of being unwanted.' It was a lesson she'd learned from her own experience, and what prompted her to give up her relatively comfortable job as headmistress of a Calcutta convent school to work alongside the city's poorest slum-dwellers in the late 1940s and the region's lepers a decade later. Even stronger than her desire to bring food to the hungry and healing to the sick was her tireless ambition to communicate to everyone she met that they mattered.

It's a much-needed message, anywhere in the world. A few years ago, one of Britain's leading high street banks ran a television advert, inspired by the film *Blade Runner*, showing a frustrated bank customer in a highly mechanized future fighting his way past impersonal machines into the office of his bank manager, only to find that the manager himself is also a machine – a very human-looking android, but one totally incapable of a personal touch. 'I just want to *talk* to someone,' cried the distraught customer. It was a cry that echoed far more widely than just bank customers. As the traditional bonds of family and community disappear, with them exits that personal touch.

When Henry Ford launched his famous Model T, the first car ever to be made on a construction line, he

informed customers just what kind of personalized service
they could expect from the Ford Motor Company. 'You can
have any colour you want,' he assured prospective buyers,
'as long as it's black!'

All too many people feel that society, and perhaps especially the welfare system, gives them the same level of
impersonalized service. 'You can be any kind of person
and have any kind of help you want,' society seems to tell
them, 'so long as it's this!' One size fits all. For those
dependent on the welfare system, this is a kind of double
whammy. Not only is their individuality and importance
crushed by poverty and deprivation, it's then also denied
by the very instruments and institutions that are supposed
to help them out of their vicious circle. Large bureaucracies
often end up hurting the very people they were set up to
help.

The answer to depersonalizing poverty, therefore, can't
be an impersonal state welfare machine. That's why the
top priority of any effective welfare provider – one that
helps people out of their situation of dependency rather
than keeping them dependent – has to be enabling people
to see their own intrinsic value and importance.

Poverty and deprivation aren't conditions people can
just pull themselves out of by their own bootstraps. It's far
more complicated than that. People will often get caught in
a downward spiral that sucks them deeper and deeper into
poverty and despair, like a powerful vortex. There's a kind
of system in place that tends to favour those on top, which
is why, left unchecked, the poor usually get poorer while
the rich get richer.

You can see this system in place in games like Monopoly.

Next time you play the game, wait until all the properties have been snapped up, and then swap positions. However good a Monopoly player you are, if you inherit the hand of a player who only managed to buy Old Kent Road and the Water Works, while the hand you give up to someone else included the complete Mayfair and Bond Street sets, you're going to lose. Players who inherit poor hands find it considerably harder to stay in the game than those who inherit good ones. It takes extraordinary skill and judgement to pull back from the brink of liquidation if you own little property and no houses. By contrast, it takes almost no skill at all to win if you've inherited more houses and hotels than anyone else.

The important thing to realize, however, is that this vicious circle doesn't just operate in terms of people's financial situation. Poverty isn't just a material problem – it's a spiritual and emotional one too. Clambering back out of the quagmire of poverty and depression when all you seem to have been dealt are the spiritual and emotional equivalents of Old Kent Road and the Water Works can seem almost impossible, and it's even worse if you know that there are other people depending on you.

That's why the key to any real social transformation has to begin and end with a real personal transformation. People who feel they're unwanted and unimportant will never have the motivation and spiritual resources needed to make any effective changes to themselves or their environment.

And that's why churches and other faith-based agencies actually have an advantage when it comes to delivering effective, transforming care, because their approach to welfare begins and ends with the needs and importance of the individual. That's not to say that churches aren't interested and involved in tackling welfare problems at a social, systemic level – they are, or should be. It's just that churches know that social approaches don't work unless they're accompanied by the personal touch.

Freddie, a 30-year-old East Ender who'd spent more than a third of his life as a heroin addict, had no job, no prospects and no hope. Financing his habit had meant turning to crime, earning himself what he jokingly referred to as a 'season ticket' for police stations and prison cells. But the lowest point came for him one Christmas morning, when he woke to find that one of his flatmates was staring at his arm with a sad look in her eyes. As he glanced down, he saw that there was still a needle in there from where he'd shot up the night before. Part of him wanted to change, but he just couldn't see how. Another part of him simply didn't believe he was worth it.

It was only when a chance encounter with a member of a local church put him in touch with a Christian rehabilitation agency that things began to look brighter. It was their approach, treating him as if he really mattered, that finally triggered a real change. 'To have someone believing in you at that time was amazing – I was totally taken aback by it,' he explained. 'I think once you realize you're worth something, your whole being changes.'

This approach used to be an integral part of the kind of help and 'charity' offered (at one time almost exclusively) by faith-based groups. In the Middle Ages, 'charity' wasn't a thing bestowed by the fortunate on the less fortunate. Instead, the word was used to describe an egalitarian social relationship in which status and possessions were irrelevant. 'Charity' wasn't about giving someone a hand-out, or even a hand-up. It was about seeing them as equals, enjoying their company and appreciating their value as a human being quite apart from their wealth or position – or lack of it. It acted as a kind of moral and social leveller, rather like the 'Jubilee' principle in the Old Testament. It reminded rich people that they were, in God's eyes, no more important than poor people; and it reminded poor people that they were, in God's eyes, no less important than rich people.

The New Testament church understood this all too well. People from totally different social backgrounds – men and women, Jews and Gentiles, slaves and slave owners – met as equals when they met as the church. Not all social barriers were completely broken down, but they were put firmly in perspective. Everyone was special to God. *Everyone mattered.*

And it's this radical perspective that drives us, as churches and Christian charities, to get – and stay – involved in welfare provision today. We may not talk much about our faith to those we help, but our under-standing that they, just as much as we, are special to God is what motivates us to care. And it's this message that people *matter*, whether we phrase it in the language of faith or not, that will form the bedrock of change.

Not just personal change either, but real social change too. Because when people start to understand that they matter, they start to understand that others matter as well. And that means that when people are helped by faith-based agencies and go through a real personal transformation in which they begin to realize their own importance, they stop being part of the problem and start instead to become part of the solution. A vicious circle is turned into a virtuous circle.

In other words, not only are individuals themselves transformed by the approach of faith-based groups, but they also help to transform others in their turn. The wheels of genuine social transformation begin to turn.

3. Faith in the Future

Rooted, sustainable, committed, imaginative, transforming solutions to seemingly intractable problems – this is what local churches and Christian charities offer in terms of welfare provision. All in all, it's a pretty impressive package. In fact, it's no exaggeration to say that it's changed the face of a nation on more than one occasion in the last 50 years alone.

Take the civil rights movement in the USA, for example. It's easy to forget just how much of a faith-based movement this really was. It was so phenomenally successful, and in the intervening years has been so universally praised, that we tend to lose sight of the fact that the cornerstone of the whole thing was local churches. While 'secular' authorities at national and sometimes even local levels dithered about what could realistically be done to end the dehumanizing system of Segregation in the South, local churches and church leaders got on and did something. Many national leaders talked a great talk – President John F. Kennedy, for instance, famously claimed that civil rights legislation was a mere 'stroke of the pen' away (a stroke he somehow never managed to make) – but it was the churches who actually *walked* the talk . . . sometimes literally.

It's no coincidence that the majority of those who struggled, and even died, during the campaign were men, women and children with a clear and totally committed faith.

- Churches offered a ready-made and entirely *rooted* network for both vital community welfare and effective political protest. It was the only one available to African Americans at the time.

- Faith offered *sustainable*, long-term, non-violent approaches to obtaining civil rights – ones that could, in the words of Martin Luther King, 'transform an enemy into a friend'.

- Christians and those of other faiths (like Michael Schwerner and Andrew Goodman, the two young Jewish activists whose murder in 1963, along with local church member James Chaney, formed the basis of the film *Mississippi Burning*) showed absolute, unswerving, faith-driven *commitment* through all the ups and downs, trials and tribulations of a harsh, decade-long struggle for freedom, justice and respect.

- From bus boycotts and freedom rides to sit-ins and city marches, the faith-based campaign was consistently inventive and *imaginative* in its effort to bring about a peaceful end to an institutionalized and emotionally deep-set racism, finding new ways around entrenched problems that had baffled the establishment for years.

- Above all, however, the Christian-inspired civil rights campaign was successful because it was capable of *transforming* both individuals and society. At one and the same time, it tackled the system *and* the people who profited and lost by it. African Americans learned to appreciate their own importance, identity and worth, inspiring them to stop being victims and to challenge the system. At the same time, former white racists slowly began to see their own importance, identity and worth in ways that didn't depend on the oppression of others. Real social transformation began and ended with real personal transformation.

And the impetus for the whole thing? The key ingredient that gave it its content, character, consistency and commitment? Faith.

> *Every human society is governed by assumptions, normally taken for granted. . . There is no such thing as an ideological vacuum.*
> Lesslie Newbigin, former missionary and theologian

The tragedy of discrimination

Why is it, then, that time after time churches and Christian charities, along with other faith-based groups, find themselves being discriminated against for no reason other than their religious conviction?

Ram Gidoomal, one of the independent candidates in

London's historic 2000 mayoral elections, encountered this discrimination at a key stage in his campaign. When he submitted a Party Election Broadcast to the BBC, as he was entitled to do as an official candidate, Ram was informed in stark terms that the public service broadcaster would not be showing his tape on air. He was mystified. So was a top national newspaper, which took it upon itself to find out the reason for Ram's disqualification. What it discovered was extraordinary. The name of Ram's party was the Christian People's Alliance. 'We don't like the word "Christian",' a BBC official explained to the newspaper. 'It's as simple as that.'

More often than not, however, it's statutory bodies that do the discriminating, and in a wide variety of ways. When Oasis recently approached one of London's borough councils to talk about the possibility of working together to set up a 'foyer' for homeless people, we had a real uphill struggle convincing some of the council's key players that we were both able and appropriate partners. A number of prominent council officials didn't like the fact that we were Christians, and they allowed that seriously to colour their initial judgements about our basic competence and suitability. Forget 'presumed innocent'. From the word go we had to mount a real defence against anti-Christian prejudice.

Some council officials thought that a joint venture could never happen with any real degree of success; others thought it *should* never happen. Eventually it did. Today, the foyer, managed by Oasis, houses 18 young people and provides IT training for up to 500 others per year. As promised, we'd mobilized thousands of young people from local churches to raise funds and awareness in the community, and in highly imaginative ways. To their great credit, most of the council officials who had expressed either doubt or flat denial that it could or should be done have thrown their support behind us enthusiastically now that it's up and running. But I'll never forget the senior administrator who, after seeing the project video – made by the young people themselves, giving a behind-the-scenes look at their phenomenal fundraising efforts and the faith motivation that inspired them – asked if he could have a copy for his own promotional use . . . but with all the 'Christian bits' cut out!

> *People* are *what they believe.*
> Anton Chekov, Russian playwright

It's a prejudice encountered time after time in every corner of the land. Churches and other Christian groups constantly find themselves being attacked or passed over for funding and other resources because of their faith. And all in the name of religious tolerance! 'There are none so intolerant as the tolerant', as the saying goes. I was recently discussing plans for a new church-based educational initiative with a senior figure in a different London council, and he told me in no uncertain terms that 'parents in our borough aren't at all happy with Christian-based education'. But the truth is, the local parents have no objections. In fact, all of the existing local church schools are so popular and inundated with applications that they have waiting lists for places. Why? Because parents know that a specifically Christian school generally offers the best-value education. In fact, it seems that the only people who aren't happy with my proposal are the decision-makers in the local statutory bodies. For them, the merits of faith aren't up for debate, or even on the radar.

Public values

As a senior figure in the Church of England puts it, 'The biggest problem facing the church today is persuading yesterday's avant-garde that they're yesterday's avant-garde.' A lot of those people now in positions of power and influence grew up in the 1960s and were educated to believe, as a matter of strict dogma, that faith, spirituality and religion were dead. But not only are faith and spirituality very much alive, interest in them is growing fast. Faith is alive and well in twenty-first-century Britain. In fact, the only thing likely to be buried in the near future is the anachronistic idea that faith is dead.

Part of the problem is that most of those people who oppose Christian projects because they're Christian imagine that if a project has no explicit basis of faith or values, it therefore comes value-free. But the truth is that nothing comes value-free. As Lesslie Newbigin pointed out, the myth that in public life we can rely on totally objective facts and opinions, entirely neutral and unencumbered by anyone's personal subjective values or bias, has come under serious attack. The idea that God either doesn't exist or shouldn't stick his nose into particular issues – that religious opinions have no bearing on public life – is itself a subjective religious opinion. Atheism (the belief that God doesn't exist) and practical atheism (the belief that God might as well not exist) are just as much religious, spiritual faith opinions as theism (the belief that God exists and gets involved in human affairs).

A friend of mine runs a well-established, highly regarded Christian youth initiative. He was recently asked by a local council to renew his contract to place youth workers with a project in a deprived inner-city area. He was surprised by the request, as he'd had to work so hard to get the contract in the first place because of an initial hesitancy about using Christian youth workers. 'Yes,' they explained, 'we were initially uneasy that Christians might exert an undue influence on the young people. But the thing about your guys is, they're clear about there being a difference between right and wrong. Many of the workers we've had in the past have tried so hard to be PC and neutral over moral issues that the young people have failed to grasp that moral choices have real and lasting consequences. But your team sends out the message that right and wrong *matter*. And they have values worth copying.'

It's a tiny ray of hope. And it's one that seems to have found a very occasional echo elsewhere. My friend J. John recently found his public talks on the Ten Commandments being enthusiastically supported by one local council, which similarly valued his emphasis on the fact that moral choices have serious consequences; that there's a real and important difference between right and wrong.

Tragically, examples like this are all too rare, and entirely dependent on individuals at a local level being open-minded enough to see past prejudice and begin to grasp the nettle of partnership. But when, we need to ask, can we look forward to seeing more consistency and co-operation? When will churches and Christian charities that provide welfare be judged on the merits and outcomes of their work rather than on someone else's biased evaluation of their doctrinal basis of faith?

> *The Third Way recognizes the limits of government in the social sphere, but also the need for government, within those limits, to forge new partnerships with the voluntary sector.*
> Tony Blair, Prime Minister

A growing political commitment to change?

The good news is, there have been the beginnings of a thaw of the 'Cold War' when it comes to ideas on welfare in the halls of Westminster. In the past, left-wing politicians seemed to want to put social care almost exclusively into the hands of central government and local authorities, with as little involvement as possible from charities or other voluntary groups, while right-wing politicians seemed to want to put social care almost exclusively into the hands of charities and other voluntary groups, with as little involvement as possible from central government or local authorities. But today, both left and right are starting to talk about the need for positive and meaningful co-operation between national government and the voluntary sector. There's increasing discussion of strategic partnership: government backing charities, including churches and other faith-based agencies, in the fight against poverty.

What's brought about this sudden change of heart across the political spectrum? Why have long-held political dogmas of free market and state control now begun to melt? To some extent, the answer is that political parties at the national level have been much faster than their local counterparts in appreciating the impossibility of providing value-free services. Starting with the field of education, a few years ago national bodies began to abandon their naïve belief in unbiased and totally 'objective' provision.

But there's a second reason why the words and speeches are starting to change. To put it starkly, parties on both the left and the right have begun to wake up to the extraordinary job being done by Britain's 200,000 registered charities and 200,000 non-charitable voluntary groups, and the enormous potential to be gained by co-operation.

After so many years of tension, with the Conservatives seeing charities as a substitute for government welfare provision and Labour basically seeing them as a threat to it, this new interest in genuine partnership is welcome news.

The truth is, voluntary sector groups on the one hand and local and central government on the other can achieve a lot by working together. Why? The reason is simple: each has something of benefit to the other if it's to do its job as efficiently and effectively as possible.

- Governments and local authorities can bring a consistency to local services and a national safety net, as well as joined-up policies and the massive boon of public sector funding.
- Churches, charities and voluntary agencies can bring

what government, with its bulk and bureaucracy, can't: rooted, sustainable, committed, imaginative and transforming one-to-one action.

But it's not all plain sailing. We're encouraged by the language we hear, but it still has to translate into action for those who need it. Words, as they say, are cheap. There's a huge difference between talking about ending discrimination and improving co-operation, and actually doing these things. Speeches can be forgotten, or 're-spun' to mean something else in time. But what really matters is things changing on the ground, at a local level.

As local churches and Christian charities, in common with other faith-based agencies, there are three major traps that we need to watch out for.

The thin end of the wedge

The first danger is government, whatever its political persuasion, using the language of partnership as a Trojan horse to smuggle in tax cuts or a stiff public spending freeze. If the overall pot of gold shrinks, churches and charities will simply find themselves vainly trying to meet more needs with fewer resources. We need to beware of government dividing up welfare provision into a thousand parts, only then to cut it back. Real partnership doesn't mean rolling back the welfare state. It means improving, and in some senses actually extending, it.

Unequal partnership

The second danger is government either dumping the burden of welfare provision onto the voluntary sector, giving cash but nothing else, or putting endless discriminatory conditions on their co-operation. There's a real tension here. On the one hand, genuine partnership doesn't mean offloading troubles onto charities. It means empowering them to do an even better job by linking them in to an overall strategy that uses their skills and resources to the full. It's no good charities having full access to funds if key areas of government policy then directly undermine the good work they're doing with those funds. Partnership entails open discussion both ways, helping to ensure that individual projects and national policies work together to solve highly complex problems.

On the other hand, genuine partnership doesn't entail government using the language of partnership and national policies to squash dissent and diversity among voluntary agencies. Churches and Christian charities shouldn't have to sell their souls and become yes-men just to get access to the government ear and the public purse. Partnership means independent bodies discussing perspectives, respecting differences and working together on the basis of common ground, not complete capitulation.

All words, no action

The third danger is government using the language of partnership to disguise what historian Sir James Mackintosh once described as 'masterly inactivity'. If the apparent change in thinking at the top doesn't filter down to grass-roots policies and practice, it won't make any difference. In other words, though we applaud the rhetoric, we also need to look extremely carefully to see that steps are being taken, or at the very least promised, to ensure that the rhetoric becomes reality. 'Don't just tell us what you're going to do,' we need to say. 'Tell us how you plan to achieve it. Give us some proof that you're serious, and you're not just talking about change but are actively working on how to implement it.' Concrete measures need to be in place to guarantee that the discrimination against churches and other faith-based agencies isn't allowed to continue, but that faith-based groups are given the support and encouragement they need. Real partnership doesn't mean using the right buzzwords. It means actively working together to reach a common goal. A wise government will strive to create an environment in which the work of local churches can thrive.

We will end the growing danger of religious discrimination against religious organizations by grant-giving and regulatory bodies. A project's religious character is often the reason for the success of that project. When we make faith-based communities dilute their religious ethos to apply for grants, we endanger these energetic projects.
William Hague, Conservative Leader

Level playing field

All that churches are asking for is a level playing field. It isn't right that faith-based organizations should be excluded from the possibility of partnerships and funding simply because of their religious beliefs.

When a south coast local authority decided to mark the new millennium by building a special Millennium Hall, it announced that this state-of-the-art community centre could be booked by any group that wanted to use it – any group, that is, except specifically Christian ones. The council seemed unaware of the irony of a hall built to celebrate the 2,000th year after Christ's birth being out of bounds to any group that consciously identified itself with Christ. It seemed unaware of the hypocrisy of an organization committed to a policy of 'equal opportunities' denying those equal opportunities to Christians, as if 'all groups are equal, but some are more equal than others'. And it seemed unaware of the injustice of discriminating against people for no other reason than their religious convictions, especially when those convictions still form a major part of the backbone of our society.

That's what the *Faithworks Campaign* is all about. We're not asking for special deals, just equal opportunities. We're not asking for the red carpet treatment, just a fair and unprejudiced approach. We want to ensure that organizations with an explicit faith basis are given the same respect and resources as organizations without an explicit faith basis. And we want to ensure that this happens at a local, practical, day-to-day level, not just in the mouths of Westminster's politicians.

We don't want to monopolize welfare provision. We're not trying to ensure that all council- or quango-recognized care facilities are Christian facilities, or even faith-based facilities. We just want to see the best being done. We want to see statutory bodies using their resources and funds to support projects that really work; that offer true value for money and the best quality of service to the community.

We're in favour of diversity – horses for courses. A

friend of mine remembers opening his front door one evening to find one of his distant relatives standing there, bedraggled and homeless, looking for a place to sleep for the night. She'd been made temporarily homeless a few days before, and the council had found her a place in a short-stay hostel. 'The thing is,' she explained, 'I had to share a dormitory with a couple of screaming women – I mean, literally *screaming*. It was really frightening. I figured I'd be safer on the street. Then I remembered that you lived around here.' She was lonely, scared and vulnerable. What she needed at the time wasn't just a roof over her head, but a safe haven, and the council's facility simply couldn't offer her that. By trying to cater for everyone, they were effectively failing to cater properly for anyone. That's why diversity pays dividends.

What the *Faithworks Campaign* is asking for is a modular approach. We want statutory organizations to talk openly with individual charities, churches and other faith-based agencies about taking on particular modules of welfare provision, or about having what they already do adopted as an official module of welfare provision. We want the fact that faith works to be recognized. Any government concerned to deliver best value has a responsibility to ensure that taxpayers' money is used by those best equipped to offer the most 'bang for each buck'. So it needs to look seriously at what specific faith-based agencies can offer, and what support they need in order to be able to offer it more effectively. Rather than discriminating against churches and Christian charities because of their faith, it needs to determine fairly whether they're qualified to provide best-quality welfare.

Churches already have meeting rooms, office space, audited financial infrastructures, accountable management, local knowledge, motivated staff and enthusiastic volunteers. And many of us have a long-existing track record of tackling issues and meeting needs. We're not standing on the sidelines waiting to be given the go-ahead; we're already playing on the pitch. According to a survey by the Evangelical Alliance:

- 50 per cent of local churches are actively working to care for elderly people and support families.
- 40 per cent are involved in giving comfort and practical help to bereaved members of the community.
- 30 per cent are committed to projects designed to bring about greater community development.
- 10 per cent run either a general advice centre or debt-counselling centre, or provide support for disabled people, housing for some sector of the community, or a service offering counselling or education about drug abuse.

When you consider that, as those statistics show, many churches are offering more than one of these kinds of provision, this is a pretty impressive track record.

In addition, local churches are actually a bigger employer than the state when it comes to professional youth work. Comparing figures produced by Christian Research last year with the DfEE's official 1998 Audit of England's Youth Service, churches employ well over twice as many full-time paid youth workers as local authorities. What's more, Christian groups are actively involved in professionally training youth workers to a national occupational standard, and not just specifically for churches – up to a fifth of the London graduates of Oasis' Youth Ministry Course are working in the state sector.

That's why it is so short-sighted for local or national statutory bodies to discriminate against local churches and other faith-based voluntary groups because of their creed. Far more could be achieved if only authorities on the ground could learn to see past their prejudice and to value and respect what faith-based agencies can and already do do.

Charities in a sense are the conscience of the nation and we must be allowed to follow our consciences. We should get funding on the basis of whether our projects make a difference. Money should not be contingent on agreeing with government policies.
Shaks Ghosh, Chief Executive of Crisis

Funding and criteria

To make this happen – to ensure that faith-based groups get real access to existing and future resources – all of the major political parties need to commit themselves now, before the next General Election and the subsequent busyness and distractions of government, to developing failsafe, concrete ways of guaranteeing local churches and other faith-based agencies their fair share of funding and support at both national and local levels. It's not just about the money, of course, but funding is important.

It's all too easy for the criteria by which local and national statutory bodies determine an agency's eligibility for
grants to be skewed to the big disadvantage of faith-based
agencies. When one central London authority invited a
mid-sized, highly skilled local church to apply for statutory funding for one of its existing welfare projects as part
of the council's equal opportunities approach, church leaders found to their dismay that so many strings and conditions were being attached to the funding offer that they
couldn't, in all good conscience, accept. It would have
meant denying who and what they were: selling their
souls and turning themselves from a local church into
something more like a secular humanist group.

'It reminds me of voter registration in the days of US
Segregation,' one commentator noted. 'Black people were
legally allowed to vote, but in order to get onto the voter
register, they had to pass all kinds of locally imposed tests
that white people didn't. The questions were designed to
make sure that hardly any black people got onto the register. It was ugly, but effective. That's what we were seeing
here. The equal opportunities rhetoric says one thing, but
the locally imposed conditions mean that the reality is
something altogether different.'

Consequently, the *Faithworks Campaign* is asking local
churches to call on political parties to ensure that any
incoming government, of whichever party, not only enacts
legislation to guarantee that faith-based agencies aren't
discriminated against on the ground because of their religious beliefs, but also takes two additional key steps.

Establish clear, outcome-related funding criteria

'It's a golden rule', wrote the eighteenth-century scholar Lichtenberg, 'not to judge people by their opinions, but rather by what their opinions make of them.' To ensure that local churches and other faith-based agencies aren't discriminated against in the bid for funding, appropriate criteria need to be in place across the board. These should focus on cost-effectiveness and outcomes, not whether or not a charity or organization is sufficiently 'on message' with national or local government policy. If they make good use of the money to cause a real difference in the local community and a real dent in the problem, then whether or not they can sign up to one party manifesto or another should be entirely irrelevant. Criteria to be met by successful grant applicants could include:

- Tailoring help as much as possible to individual needs.
- Tackling dependency by boosting self-confidence and teaching life skills.
- Challenging recipients to stretch their perceived limits.
- Fostering one-to-one relationships between givers and receivers.
- Developing links with, and support from, the local community.
- Mobilizing volunteers effectively from the local community.
- Utilizing the professional skills and resources of staff and volunteers.
- Demanding real accountability and responsibility of staff.

- Quantifying success rates, with measurable medium- and long-term outcomes.
- Proving cost-effectiveness and sound financial practices.

Centrally monitor local delivery

To ensure fair and consistent implementation, central government needs to commit itself to monitoring the implementation of the above funding criteria on the ground by local or national statutory bodies when they allocate funds to voluntary groups.

Together, these two steps of establishing clear, outcome-related funding criteria and centrally monitoring local delivery should help to ensure not only that religious discrimination in funding becomes a thing of the past, but also that voluntary groups such as local churches and Christian charities don't find themselves constantly having to repackage what they do and tailor grant applications to fit in with new twists and turns in government policy. Government may change every five years or so, but the ongoing task of voluntary organizations continues.

Of course, outcomes will in a broad way still need to fit in with government strategy, simply to ensure that all the horses are pulling in roughly the same direction rather than pulling each other apart. Churches and voluntary groups need to recognize that medium-term (and even short-term) achievements are very important – governments have to be able to show real results for their time in office, otherwise electors (including members of those same churches and voluntary groups) will vote them out for failing to do enough to tackle the problems. But at the same time, governments need to recognize that real solutions and real transformations aren't like a 100-metre sprint. They're more like a marathon, and churches and charities can't keep running if the rules keep changing every few miles.

So the kinds of outcome demanded by the funding criteria and insisted on by the monitoring process need to demonstrate that appropriate intermediate goals are being met as part of an ongoing, long-term, positive, cost-effective, best quality project. There are no quick fixes when addressing the deep, underlying problems of those people dependent on welfare.

As they say, for every complex and intractable problem, there's a straightforward, simple and instant answer . . . and it's always wrong.

4. A Two-Way Street

A guaranteed end to religious discrimination at ground level, leading to strategic partnerships with both local and national statutory bodies in order to provide best-quality, cost-effective, socially transforming care and welfare is our aim.

Society needs the safety net that only a comprehensive welfare system can provide. However, we need to ensure that rather than permanently entangling those who use it, it's one that enables people to get back on their feet as quickly as possible. The task is always to challenge and empower; as one commentator put it, 'To provide a safety net that turns into a trampoline, not a hammock.'

Local churches and Christian charities are well placed and well suited to provide this kind of bounce-back welfare. Our rooted, sustainable, committed, imaginative, transforming approach – putting the emphasis firmly (but not exclusively) on flexible one-to-one attention and care – makes us ideal candidates as partners for both central and local government.

That is why we are calling for a level playing field. It is why we are asking that firm, concrete measures are taken to ensure that we're given fair and appropriate access to statutory funds, and that the work we're already doing as care providers is given the respect it deserves.

But it's no good making these demands if we don't at the same time make sure that we take steps to put our own house in order. It's not just government and local councils that need to walk the talk. Any healthy relationship needs to be a two-way street.

As local churches and Christian charities, we must recommit ourselves to developing the following.

- A *deeper understanding* of, and insight into, the problems facing society, and a deeper level of awareness of people's needs in every area of life, not just the 'spiritual'.

- A *greater degree of empathy* and sensitivity to people's pain, and a deeper respect for their opinions, especially when they're different from our own.

- A *strengthened commitment* to providing practical, personal, tailored and challenging (but unconditional) care at the point of need.

- A *more prayerful partnership* with both local and national government, praying more effectively *for* them and engaging more strategically *with* them.

- A *higher level of professionalism* and efficiency, combining genuine know-how with a fervent and heartfelt compassion.

- A *more holistic approach*, recognizing that welfare isn't a warm-up round to evangelism, but is in its own right a powerful and essential way of putting our faith into action.

Christian asceticism called the world evil and abandoned it. Humanity is waiting for a Christian revolution which will call the world evil and change it.
Walter Rauschenbusch, theologian

1. A deeper understanding

The twentieth century saw a real struggle for much of the church to recover the link between the gospel and social action. Now, as a new millennium dawns, the challenge is for us to reconcile the gospel with social justice. We need to reconnect the problems with the underlying issues, challenging the causes as well as the effects.

But if we in the church have to work hard to deepen our awareness and perception of the root problems (reconnecting symptoms with causes) we've also got to work just as hard at finding solutions, and that will almost certainly mean exploring new ground for many of us, especially when it comes to thinking through causes, symptoms and solutions from a political and social perspective. I was always taught that religion and politics don't mix. I've learned that the opposite is true: religion and politics *must* mix.

In the past, as churches, we've tended to focus our attention on the personal and individual aspects of evil. As a result, we've failed to see its corporate expressions in the structures we live with. But the truth is, by doing this we've actually, without realizing it, bought into a false dualistic division between the public world of facts and the personal and private world of values. In essence, we've privatized faith and prophecy, and tragically that leaves people with the impression that the gospel has little relevance to public life. God may have lots still to say to the church, we imply, but he has nothing to say to the rest of the world . . . except, perhaps, 'Join the church!'

This, of course, means that we inevitably end up just dabbling in community affairs, focusing on just one or two important but isolated issues in what is, in the end, a disjointed response. Instead, we must rediscover the Christ who fearlessly speaks to the social, economic and political realm with disturbing effect. We can't afford to privatize prophecy and apply it merely to the church, as if the world God loves so much (John 3:16) doesn't matter. As Walter Wink notes, 'Our task is to work to change structures as well as individuals.' It isn't a question of either/or: either individual causes and solutions or social causes and solutions. It's more a case of both/and.

The gospel has just as much to say to us as a society as it does to us as individuals; just as much to say about politics as it does about people. And just as we mustn't reduce the gospel to something one-dimensional, neither must we reduce the causes of society's problems or our proposed solutions to something one-dimensional. That's why we have to recommit ourselves to deepening our understanding of, and insight into, the problems facing society . . . and our awareness of people's needs in every area of life, not just the individual and spiritual.

We have reduced Christianity into a religion that brings
people to use the right language and to use the right words
instead of compassionately identifying with people's needs. We
have made Christianity into a lifestyle of middle class
propriety instead of a call to have one's heart broken by the
things that break the heart of Jesus.
Tony Campolo, American sociologist and Baptist
minister

2. A greater degree of empathy

A few years ago I had the privilege of meeting an extraordinary lady, a real unsung Mother Teresa, in the enormous
house she owned in the sleepy suburbs of a major city. She
ran the house as a refuge for women and children who had
suffered domestic violence. She had given up her job as
one of the city's most respected headteachers in order to
provide respite care for women and children who so des-
perately needed it.

When I asked what had motivated her to make such a
dramatic change in her lifestyle – abandoning a career
she'd spent many years pursuing – she explained that the
school where she had been headmistress had been in a
very run-down, problem-laden area. Half the houses in the
catchment had been boarded up, and pupils had regularly
had to walk past burnt-out cars on their way to school. It
was a tough job, but she'd relished the challenge of trying
to educate and inspire her pupils, often with little or no
active support from parents. Then, one day, a six-year-old
boy had come to school after several days' unexplained

absence. 'Why were you away?' she'd asked sternly. She was used to children missing school and had thought she'd heard every reason in the book. But the story that emerged had shocked her to the core. The boy's father had taken a gun to his head and shot himself . . . with his young son sitting on his lap. The experience had opened her eyes to what many children in her school went through at home, especially in terms of domestic violence, and the more she'd found out, the more her heart had been broken and the more she'd felt compelled to do something about it. In the end, she'd resigned her headship and founded her refuge, working to restore the lives and brittle self-confidence of some of the city's brutalized women and children. 'God gives the desolate a home to live in,' Psalm 68:6 (NRSV) assures us. This courageous lady went and did likewise.

For me, her experience is a stark reminder of just how easy it is for us to miss what's really going on around us, and how deeply it can affect people. And it underlined to me once more just how crucial a factor empathy is in helping people come to terms with their troubles and loss. There was no magic formula at the house, no twelve-step programme – just time, space, peace and industrial amounts of sensitivity and understanding. And it worked.

'Love anything,' wrote C. S. Lewis, 'and your heart will certainly be wrung, and possibly be broken.' In fact, if our care and action doesn't flow from a real heart-wringing empathy then, in Paul's words, it's merely 'a resounding gong or a clanging symbol' (1 Corinthians 13:1). Like the other prominent New Testament church leaders, Paul understood that the most appropriate and effective action overflows from a deep sense of care and compassion. He knew the transforming power of a giving rooted in love, even when you don't think you have very much to give. He knew that churches had to be first and foremost communities that cared. It was their task, in essence, to act as a kind of extended family.

This way of being church was one he had inherited from his Jewish roots and his understanding of the role of the synagogue. We tend to think of the synagogues of the New Testament era as being a bit like the popular stereotype of modern-day churches – places to go on the sabbath for your weekly dose of 'word and worship'. Although synagogues did hold services, they were almost incidental to their function. The main week-by-week, day-by-day Jewish worship took place not in the synagogue, nor even in Jerusalem's Temple (which would have struck us as being more abattoir than abbey!), but in the family home.

Of course, New Testament era Jewish families weren't the shrunken nuclear nest of today: mum, dad, two point four children and a hamster! They were extended, gathering together all kinds of relatives and even friends. The family was a rich, inclusive environment: a place not only of worship but also of entertainment; of physical, emotional and spiritual sustenance. It provided nurture for the young, nursing for the sick, comfort for the brokenhearted, company for the lonely-hearted, rest for the weary and a home when retirement came. It was the source of both identity and social security in the ancient Jewish world.

Synagogues gradually arose as a kind of second tier of extended family, acting to knit together individual families

– and all those widows, orphans and foreigners without a family of their own to support them – into a real caring community. Especially in the bustling pagan cities of the ancient Mediterranean like Tarsus, where Paul grew up, the 'second skin' of a synagogue could be not just a life-saver, but a social transformer. That's why early churches were more like messianic synagogues than our modern-day church establishments.

It's an approach and emphasis we'll have to work hard to nurture if we're to continue to stand out as effective welfare providers. Care born of genuine empathy and belonging has the power to transform and rebuild communities, while care without empathy will never generate anything more than dependency and despondency.

I hereby pledge myself – my person and my body – to . . . meditate daily on the teachings and life of Jesus . . . ; walk and talk in the manner of love, for God is love . . . ; pray daily to be used by God in order that all men might be free.
Pledge signed by civil rights demonstrators at a sit-in in Birmingham, Alabama, 1963

We need to learn to be inclusive not exclusive, accepting not excepting, transforming not conforming. We increasingly need to take the kind of long-term approach to other people's spiritual and emotional development that God takes with our own. The care we give has to do more than just salve our consciences. As a result, we need to increase our sensitivity to people's pain, and our respect for their opinions (especially when they're different from our own) in the knowledge that, as Paul remarked, if we don't have love, we don't have anything at all.

To put it simply: both our projects and our churches themselves need to be genuinely inspirational communities where care precedes creed and belonging precedes believing.

3. A strengthened commitment

When Scotland's Iona Community gather for morning prayer each day, their conventional service has an unconventional ending. In fact, to be precise, it has no ending at all. Unlike most worship services, there's no blessing or 'benediction' – until the end of the evening service. Instead, community members go about their daily tasks as if these were in themselves a continuation of the worship service, which they are! There's no hard distinction between worship and work, liturgy and life. Nor should there be. The community's members are as committed to real hands-on action in pursuit of justice and peace as they are to a life of daily prayer and Bible reading, but they don't see one as secular and the other as sacred. Instead, they see everything they do in life – politics or prayer – as a form of worship and service.

In recent years the national youth event Soul Survivor has tried to emulate this kind of approach. A few years ago I was asked to speak and I was given the brief of tackling the issue of mission and service. Knowing that the evening talks were followed by a time of ministry, I got the full backing of the organizers to have a time of 'ministry with a difference'. As I told the crowd of enthusiastic and highly committed young people who were all crammed into the arena, Christian ministry is primarily about giving not getting, serving not being served. As St Francis of Assisi prayed, 'Grant that [we] may not so much seek to be consoled as to console, to be understood as to understand, to be loved as to love, for it is in giving that we receive, it is in pardoning that we are pardoned, and it is in dying that we are born to eternal life.' That night, thousands of young people came forward and discovered for themselves the truth of Jesus' words 'It is more blessed to give than to receive' (Acts 20:35). We'd even brought along a three-ton truck as a portable 'altar' for the occasion, and by the end of the evening the truck was full of clothes for distribution through the Oasis Health Centre – some of them new, many of them designer branded, all of them in good condition. That winter, some of London's homeless people found themselves the proud owners of good quality D & G, Adidas or Calvin Klein clothes, and Reebok, Nike or Kickers footwear.

Last summer, Soul Survivor took this a step further. As part of Message 2000, young people spent a week learning to see the close connection between worship and work. After a morning of teaching came an afternoon of back-breaking work. Over two weeks, the Manchester district of Swinton found itself with a thousand enthusiastic volunteers (500 young people a week) getting involved in everything from painting houses to planting gardens and clearing rubbish. The Greater Manchester Police, for whom it had apparently been something of a no-go area, told us later that for those two weeks crime had not only dropped in Swinton, it had actually stopped altogether! A superintendent apparently asked if the young people could stay in the area, and their efforts even received a ringing endorsement from William Hague in his speech a couple of months later to the Charities Aid Foundation.

What makes style-conscious young people part with their designer gear? What makes a generation schooled to be consumers rebel against the system and spend a week getting their hands dirty, literally, in a run-down part of Manchester? To put it simply: their faith. They were learning that work itself is a potent form of worship, enabling them to 'offer [their] bodies as living sacrifices, holy and pleasing to God' as an act of what Paul called real spiritual worship (Romans 12:1). As a result, they found that their commitment to providing real community welfare, with no strings attached, reached new levels.

When St Paul says, 'Come out and be separate,' he did not mean that Christians ought to take no interest in anything on earth except religion. To neglect science, art, literature and politics – to read nothing which is not directly spiritual – to know nothing about what is going on among mankind, and never to look at a newspaper – to care nothing about the government of one's own country, and to be utterly indifferent to the persons who guide its counsels and make its laws – all this may seem very right and proper in the eyes of some people. But I take leave to think that it is an idle, selfish neglect of duty.

J. C. Ryle, nineteenth-century Bishop of Liverpool

As local churches, we need to increase our existing commitment to offering unconditional care and welfare. If our welfare work is to be effective, we need to work hard at intensifying our pledge to provide practical, personal, tailored and challenging (but unconditional) care at the point of need. And to do that, we need to allow God to deepen our faith.

4. A more prayerful partnership

Five years after becoming an MP in 1780 at the age of 21, William Wilberforce became a committed Christian. For a while he considered abandoning his political career in favour of working as a missionary or a minister, but he changed his mind when he saw that he could, as historian Asa Briggs puts it, 'save souls through the medium of political action'. In 1787 he started a lifelong campaign against both slavery and a vast range of other social problems, from promoting Bible knowledge and keeping Sunday 'holy' to preventing cruelty to children or animals and eradicating poverty. With a complex web of joined-up strategies and working partnerships, both religious and political, he laboured tirelessly to turn his dream into reality.

Wilberforce epitomized an attitude of prayerful, persistent pragmatism. His long fight in Parliament to abolish slavery throughout the British Empire, for example, lasted 38 years, and stopped only when ill health forced him to retire from public office. (He died one month before the Slavery Abolition Act was finally passed, in 1833.) On the way, he found himself working alongside people with agendas radically different from his own – Quakers, for example, who otherwise saw him as being far too conservative, and the followers of Adam Smith, whose objection to slavery was on the purely economic grounds that its running costs were far too high. Wilberforce's ideals were a major force in the drive for abolition, and he never stopped praying for both supporters and opponents, but without his hard-nosed political realism and his willingness to work alongside those with whom he often clashed in other areas, his plans would have come to nothing. His willingness to compromise was a key factor in his phenomenal success.

As local churches, this is the kind of example we need to copy, both praying more effectively *for* and engaging more effectively *with* local and national government as sincere, strategic partners. We don't have to agree totally with everyone we work with, any more than they have to agree with us point for point on our approach. Ability to compromise in the short term is a key component in any successful working relationship.

In fact, of course, it cuts both ways. The more we can learn to accept people and work with them on their own terms, the more credibility and leverage we'll have when we demand that they accept and work with us on *our* own terms. One of the distinguishing marks of any Christian organization, from local churches to charities, is our commitment to prayer. Without this, we lose one of the main planks of our identity as a specifically Christian agency, not to mention a key element in our effectiveness. It's not something we impose on others, for example insisting that our meetings with council officials begin with five minutes of head-down, eyes-closed fervent intercession, but it *is* something we strongly believe helps us to become more focused, more committed, more enthusiastic and more in tune with God and one another.

So when statutory bodies refuse to respect our right to pray, or discriminate against us under the guise of 'equal opportunities' because we insist that prayer is an integral part of what we do, they act unfairly. And when they refuse to work with us because we're Christian, they act irresponsibly, especially in view of their mandate to provide the kind of best quality, cost-effective care we can help them with. But by the same token we act unfairly and irresponsibly when we refuse to work with them because they *don't* pray or *aren't* Christian. We may not approve of their values any more than they approve of our faith and prayer, but we're foolish and hypocritical if we let that stand in the way of the kind of pragmatic partnership that can get the job done.

When I was a minister in Tonbridge, the church and the local social services pioneered a very effective strategic partnership – a kind of job-share. One of the church members, Barry, was a qualified and highly experienced social worker, and the church and council agreed to a joint-funding arrangement by which he worked in the church's specific geographical 'patch' under the auspices of both the council and the church. The council recognized that Barry was professional enough not to push his faith on his clients, and that the church respected their position and opinions enough not to encourage him to try. The council also knew that the church offered a unique blend of back-up facilities and inroads into the local community. At the same time, the church recognized that local people had needs that Barry could help meet as a social worker, and that we and the council had a mutual interest in supporting his work.

This is the kind of partnership that we need to be more involved in as local churches and Christian charities. It's the kind of partnership practised by Wilberforce and Shaftesbury. And it's similar to the kind of pragmatic working arrangement adopted in the Old Testament by characters such as Joseph, Daniel and Nehemiah, who served the pagan kings of Egypt, Babylon, Medea and Persia. Not only should we pray in an informed way for our local authorities and other organizations, but, as far as we can in all good conscience, we should work alongside them as strategic partners.

The English think incompetence is the same thing as sincerity.
Quentin Crisp, New York based English writer

5. A higher level of professionalism

A couple of years ago I was invited to attend a conference, sponsored by the World Bank, on the issue of micro-industry in the Third World. I was asked to give my insights into the situation in India and the micro-industrial projects Oasis has set up in that country to combat poverty and promote development. I spoke for a short time, telling people about the work of Oasis India, then threw the floor open for questions. Most of the feedback was positive, but one World Bank official couldn't disguise her scepticism.

'The problem with your projects', she informed me, playing to the assembled crowd, 'is that they are well-meaning but often ineffective. You could do a lot more to grasp the principles of empowerment or mentoring, for example. You could be more professional.' I listened as she gently chided us for what she saw as a slightly amateur, do-gooder approach. 'Next time you're near Mumbai,' she advised me, knowing we worked there, 'take the time to visit a project that's really world class. You could learn a lot from it about how empowering, micro-industrial development work *should* be done. It's called Purnata Bhavan.'

I let a moment roll by before replying: 'And next time *you* visit Purnata Bhavan, take the time to look at the sign outside. Just below the name it says, "An Oasis Project."'

It was an extraordinary moment, but one that goes to show just how professional (or, more accurately, unprofessional) many of the people who are involved in welfare provision in secular institutions think we are! And that's the challenge: to prove that the words 'Christian' and 'incompetent' are not synonymous, boosting our professionalism and efficiency, combining genuine know-how with a fervent and heartfelt compassion.

It's ironic, of course. After all, the church was the original caring, professional, pioneering welfare before there even were any 'secular institutions'. In the Middle Ages, for example, churches and monasteries offered the only help available for those who fell through the cracks in society. And when the upheavals of the eighteenth-century Industrial Revolution destroyed in just a few generations a traditional way of life (and welfare) that had existed for hundreds of years, the church was at the forefront of attempts to stem the growing tide of poverty and outright destitution. In fact, it was only in the mid-nineteenth century. that the government and statutory organizations began to think of themselves as having any significant role to play in welfare provision, and only in the twentieth century that some politicians began to think the state should have an exclusive role to play. But even so, churches and Christian charities have certainly not bowed out. If anything, we've increased our presence and provisions.

But that's why it is such a tragedy when outdated Christian stereotypes pass for 'typical' Christian welfare providers, while a majority of efficient, effective facilities and services go totally unnoticed. Churches and Christian charities *can* do a highly professional job, and many do, day after day, up and down the country.

Even so, some deadly myths persist among churches and Christian organizations.

Size matters

Some people seem to think that only large organizations and agencies can act in a professional way. Two or three staff in an upstairs office can't possibly offer a top-notch service. But the truth is, professionalism is a state of mind. Size really *doesn't* matter. From doctors to lawyers, plumbers to builders, society is full of small firms and businesses that do a very professional job, as well as a number of big businesses that do a very unprofessional job. Exactly the same is true when it comes to welfare. Big doesn't necessarily mean beautiful.

Put your trust in God, not management structures

Some Christians seem to think it's somehow less than spiritual to take a professional approach to things. Business
procedures such as proper budgets, salaries, accountability
structures and five-year plans appear to administrate God
out of the equation. But the reality is, a professional
approach sends people the message that you care enough
to think things out fully and do a proper job. Far from hid-
ing God behind mountains of paperwork and administra-
tion, good planning demonstrates to people that God
cares. After all, God himself is a planner, an arch-strategist.
By contrast, a slap-dash 'amateur' attitude sends those in
professional welfare work the signal that Christians don't
really understand the issues, and sends those on the receiv-
ing end of welfare the signal that they're not important
enough, and that God doesn't care enough about them, to
warrant a more serious, professional approach.

A few years ago, some friends of mine moved into a house
in a very tough part of one of the UK's big cities. They
were both committed Christians, but they were also very
committed to transforming their local environment. They
knew it would be hard work, but refused to let that put
them off. One of their first actions was to help start a
Residents' Association. Slowly, they saw a drop in the rate
of crime, vandalism and drug addiction, and real improve-
ments in school attendance and community relations. After
a number of years of hard work to combat the area's problems, my friends started up a church in the community
centre. Today, not only is that church thriving, but it has a

great reputation with both local residents and the local council.

Our challenge is not to be overtaken by notions of revival, nor overwhelmed by a struggle for survival. It is to keep our eye firmly on God's enduring agenda: the transformation of our society.

Joel Edwards, General Director of Evangelical Alliance

6. A more holistic approach

It's said that when the famous classical composer Robert Schumann died, his friend Johannes Brahms, another brilliant composer, visited Schumann's widow. But on arriving at the house, he went straight to the piano, sat down, played some music and left – without muttering a single word. He couldn't find any words to express the depth of his grief, so he found the best way he knew to honour his friend and tell Mrs Schumann how he felt about her husband's death. But, of course, no words were needed. His feelings were very powerfully demonstrated without them. His presence was worth a thousand words to her. It spoke more eloquently than words could ever have done.

A friend of mine relates this story to the role of churches in much of our society today, particularly in the inner city. 'Most British people don't know much about the Christian faith,' he explains, 'but they *do* still associate churches with God. That's why the main task facing churches is to be there for people. We need to let them know by our actions and our presence that God is with them and cares about them, because actions speak much louder than words.'

As Christians, we tend to be very keen on words. In desiring to be the 'people of the word' we've become the people of many words. We see them as the gateway to faith. But while words are certainly very important, they're by no means the only way people can come to understand and respond to God's love. 'We're very unhappy about letting the actions speak for themselves,' my friend continues, 'because we want to make absolutely sure that they're communicating the right message. That's understandable. It's even commendable. The trouble is, it's not always effective. Sometimes the gospel works best when we're not trying to subtitle it all the time – when we let it run as a kind of silent movie, offering verbal insights only when people ask for them. I think what Spurgeon said of the Bible is equally true of the gospel a lot of the time: the best way to defend it is actually to give it the freedom to defend itself.'

Many local councils and other statutory bodies are fearful that Christians' only interest in welfare work is as a pretext for evangelism and recruitment. All we really care about is 'saving souls', they argue, not 'saving bodies'; Christian welfare work is the thin end of the wedge, leading inevitably and deliberately to a narrow-minded proselytism. But the truth is that our interest in welfare work stems not from a desire to recruit, but from a desire to demonstrate God's love in action. Compassion, not conversion, is the motivation for our involvement. Acting on our faith, not telling people about it, is what drives us.

It's important to be up-front about this. If our welfare

projects are nothing more than underhanded attempts to recruit members – a pretext for proselytism rather than a genuine response to human need – then we should steer well clear. For one thing, our projects themselves are likely to backfire: if those we're helping get the impression that we're being less than honest with them about both our motivation and our aim, they'll probably run a mile. And not just from us, but from God as well. By contrast, if they begin to understand and trust that we care for them as whole people, not just souls to be 'counted into the kingdom', then there's a much better chance they'll understand and trust that God cares for them as whole people too.

Our task, in other words, is to be a kind of icon of the Trinity: a visible image of the invisible God. Our welfare work isn't a warm-up round to proselytism; in its own right it's a legitimate way of incarnating God's loving presence in the community and putting our faith into action. We care for people not because we hope they'll join the church, although we'd obviously welcome that too, but because God cares for them.

When our politicians tell us that faith makes community work, do they actually mean any more than that for them faith makes community work cheaply or, more often, for free? Our message to them must be clear: we believe that the Church delivers best value for money; if you believe the same, work with us, support us and give us the resources which will enable us to deliver.
Ram Gidoomal, Chairman of Christian People's Alliance

The time has come

So, in the run-up to the next election, our message to all the political parties is simple.

As churches and Christian charities involved in welfare provision, we're constantly working to develop a deeper understanding, a greater empathy, a strengthened commitment, a more prayerful partnership, a higher level of professionalism and a more holistic approach.

What about you? What concrete steps are your party going to take to turn your words into action, policy and legislation? How will you deliver a government that works with churches, Christian charities and other faith-based organizations on the sure footing of respect and equal partnership? How will you remove the roadblocks that have created, and continue to create, discrimination? How will you overcome the problems involved in making your promised commitments work at a local level?

Now is the time to come clean, before all the busyness and distractions of government get in the way. What measures are your party going to take to prove to us that you're serious?

Nail your colours to the mast: will your party support the four points of the *Faithworks Campaign* Declaration? Will you:

- Recognize the important contribution that local churches and Christian charities have made and can make in providing welfare within the local community?
- Acknowledge the vital role that faith plays in the motivation and effectiveness of welfare programmes devel-

oped by churches and Christian charities?

- Encourage and support the work of local initiatives developing welfare in the community, including those run by churches and other faith-based organizations, through specific legislation, outcome-related monitoring and funding without unnecessary bureaucracy or cost.

- Ensure that funding criteria for government and local authority grants to projects providing welfare in the local community do not discriminate against the faith that is vital to the success of the work of churches and faith-based organizations.

If not, tell us now. We'd just like to be sure, before we ask you to represent us, that you actually *will* represent us if we vote for you. It's as simple as that.

Getting Involved in the *Faithworks Campaign*

As movie mogul Sam Goldwyn once famously said, 'A verbal contract isn't worth the paper it's written on.' That's why the *Faithworks Campaign* is committed to making sure that all the encouraging rhetoric we've been hearing from Westminster translates into reality.

There are five key areas in which you and your church can play a vital role.

1. National political action

- Sign the *Faithworks Campaign* Declaration online or by calling the *Faithworks Campaign* hotline. Get everyone in your church to sign it too. By standing together, we can make a real difference.

2. Local political action

- Write to your local MP and Prospective Parliamentary Candidates about the *Faithworks Campaign*. A draft let-ter is available online or from our hotline.

- Arrange a public ('hustings') meeting with your sitting local MP and other Prospective Parliamentary Candidates in the run-up to the next General Election. Do this as a local group of churches. Question them about their attitude to the *Faithworks Campaign*. If they are elected as your MP, how would they see their relationship with the local churches working out in practice? A briefing document giving details of how to organize a hustings meeting is available online or from our hotline.

3. Local prayer action

- Build regular 'prayer focus' times into your church's services, prayer meetings or house groups. Spend a couple of minutes briefly explaining about a problem that affects your local community (homelessness, refugees, debt, etc.) and praying in a specific and informed way for an organization that's involved in trying to solve the problem.
- Hold a special prayer meeting about a problem that affects your area, inviting an outside speaker from a local church or charity that already works to combat the problem, or perhaps even your local MP.

4. Local media action

- Contact your local newspapers, radio stations and regional TV stations. Tell them about the *Faithworks Campaign*, highlighting how it relates to your church's own welfare work.

- Produce a press release. A draft is available online or from our hotline.

- Arrange a local press conference, where local church leaders have a chance to meet and explain to the local press what the *Faithworks Campaign* is calling for and why.

5. Local community action

- Take the message of the *Faithworks Campaign* one step further: demonstrate that faith works by getting involved in the *Rebuild National Community Week* project, which is taking place in July. *Rebuild* is a pioneering initiative that enjoys the support of over 60 Christian organizations, denominations and networks. It aims to mobilize and equip local churches to make a lasting difference in their communities. A comprehensive information pack with ideas and activities is now available. Register your church today.

- Beyond the *Rebuild National Community Week*, start considering how your church can best be involved in rooted, sustainable, committed, imaginative and transforming welfare projects. Visit the *Faithworks* website for more information.

Further Information

The *Faithworks Campaign*

Visit our website on www.faithworkscampaign.org or call the *Faithworks Campaign* hotline on 020 7450 9021 for:

- The *Faithworks Campaign* Information Pack, which tells you all you need to know about how to run your local campaign.
- Copies of the *Faithworks Campaign* Declaration.
- More information about the *Rebuild National Community Week* project, and how to register.

Vision without action is hallucination. Seize the day!